Perfect Piero

~

Rose Wysocki

Table of Contents

Copyright

Publication Disclaimer

The material in this book is for informational purposes only. Since each individual situation is unique, you should use proper discretion, in consultation with a healthcare practitioner, before undertaking making or consuming any recipes in this book. The author and publisher expressly disclaim responsibility for any adverse effects including physical or mental disability or damages that may result from the use, misuse or application of the information contained in this book. The material contained in this publication is provided for information purposes only.

New Polonia Publishing

First Printing 2013
Printed in the U.S.A.

ISBN-13:978-1481992381
ISBN-10:1481992384

Dedication

For my Mother & Grandmother

Books by Rose Wysocki

Perfect Pierogi Recipes

Perfect Polish Dessert Recipes

Perfect Polish Appetizer Recipes

Introduction

I have always loved making pierogi. From the time I was a child I learned the recipes and baking methods of my Mother and Grandmother. There is a great connection to the past for me when I make the traditional dough and fillings.

I enjoyed making the traditional pierogi fillings, many of which I include in this book. After I married I experimented with more contemporary fillings. What I grew to love was combining traditional pierogi fillings with more contemporary sauces and compound butter toppings. I also enjoy combining traditional pierogi dough with contemporary fillings for an entirely new taste.

Traditional toppings for savory pierogi include melted butter, sour cream, buttered bread crumbs, caramelized onions and crisp bacon bits. For sweet pierogi the toppings include melted butter, granulated sugar, powdered sugar and sour cream topped with granulated sugar.

In this book I've also included some more contemporary toppings like homemade fruit sauces and compound butters. Fruit sauces are easily made by combining chopped fruit and sugar, cooking the mixture down and serving.

Compound butters are wonderful toppings and so easy to prepare. Just add herbs, honey or spices to softened, unsalted butter and mix well. After reforming the butter into a log and chilling it in the refrigerator, you have a delicious homemade compound butter that can be used with pierogi, hot rolls, pancakes and anything else you can think of.

In this book you'll find recipes for: 10 different pierogi doughs (traditional and contemporary), 15 savory fillings, 6 sweet fillings, 3 traditional pierogi toppings, 2 contemporary toppings, 9 compound butters and 6 sauces. I also included a list of 16 additional traditional toppings and 10 contemporary toppings (without recipes.)

Finally you'll find a lot of information about the history of pierogi, how to make pierogi dough, different methods to cut, stuff and seal the pierogi and how to cook and freeze pierogi.

This book has been a labor of love for me. I wanted to share both my wonderful pierogi recipes as well as my love for this part of my heritage.

Please Help

This is my first book and I spent so much time and effort on it because I wanted it to be as good as possible.

If you like the book could you please go to the following link and leave a review?

http://www.amazon.com/Perfect-Pierogi-Recipes-ebook/dp/B00B0GC7YK/

Thank you very much.

Rose

What are Pierogi ?

Pierogi are dumplings made of unleavened dough and are traditionally stuffed with cheese, sauerkraut, mashed potato fillings, cabbage, spinach, ground beef and fruit. Pierogi can be boiled, fried or baked. Modern Polish pierogi are semicircular or crescent-shaped.

While you can find a variety of pierogi in Poland, traditional ground meat, cabbage and mushroom pierogi is still most popular. They are usually boiled and served with melted butter and crisp bacon bits.

In Poland pierogi is the plural form of the word. People there rarely if ever use the singular form, pierog. Some say it's because pierog also refers to a Ukrainian pastry. Others say it's because no one ever wants just one pierogi! In the United States and Canada you'll often hear the plural as "pierogies."

In this book I use pierogi for both a single dumpling and for multiple dumplings.

A Brief History of Pierogi

It would be nice to know the exact moment in time that the first distinct Polish pierogi was plucked from a pan of hot butter or bacon fat and served on a plate with cooked onions, bacon bits and sour cream.   Unfortunately the exact origins of Polish pierogi are not known. In fact it's very likely the dish evolved over time.

It's speculated that an early version of a pierogi-like dumpling originated in China and were brought west across central Asia. This was probably more of a won ton like dumpling filled with vegetables.   Eventually the dumplings were introduced to Eastern Europe and spread into central Europe.

Since Poland has been conquered and occupied by different nations over the centuries, it's very possible that the Mongol invasion introduced early versions of the dumpling to eastern Europe in the mid 13th century. Eventually the early version of pierogi spread to central Europe. As the dish was adopted by each region and country, it evolved to fit the tastes and ingredients of the people in those regions.

Belarusians, Russians, Ukrainians, Poles, Czechs, Slovaks, Estonians, Latvians and Lithuanians all prepare a version of pierogi, although the name may be different.   Also each country has ethnic variations in how the dough and fillings are prepared.

For example, the Russian variety of pierogi has thicker, more bread-like dough and often contains meat. Polish and Slovak varieties have more of noodle-pastry dough and potato or cabbage fillings. Lithuanian pierogi uses dough similar to Polish pierogi but with more meat-based fillings.

Pierogi have been prepared in Poland since the thirteenth century. One story is that they first evolved as a peasant food containing potato and cabbage fillings. Over time they became popular among all social groups in Poland.

Another story states that pierogi were originally prepared and served for holidays and special occasions. Each holiday had a specific pierogi filling and shape. There was a unique pierogi served on Christmas Eve. Another different type of pierogi was served on Easter. Kurniki was a large pierogi filled with chicken that was served at weddings.

Knysze were a pierogi served only at wakes. Koladki was a special pierogi that was baked and served in January. Saniezki and Socznie were small, baked, sweet pierogi served for a person's name day. (In Poland each day has one or more names associated with it. When the day with your name arrives there is a party similar to a birthday celebration.)

These traditions with specialized pierogi in Poland have largely disappeared. However at Christmas Eve there are still two favorite pierogi served: sauerkraut & dried mushrooms and uszka, a pierogi filled with dry, wild mushrooms served in soup.

It's likely that pierogi originated as a peasant food and then the special varieties were developed over time for holidays and special occasions.

In the late 19th and early 20th centuries there was a large migration of Eastern European immigrants to the United States. They brought all of the various varieties of pierogi that were popular in their native countries. In the United States, pierogi became a very popular dish for church fundraisers and church dinners. In the 1950's pierogi eventually became more popular with other ethnic groups and the popularity continues to this day.

In both Poland and the United States, traditional pierogi fillings like potato, sauerkraut and cabbage are still popular. But you can also find many creative fillings using venison, boar, kimchi, quail eggs with caramelized onions, chicken and Mexican chili beans, lamb, rosemary and thyme etc. One of the wonderful things about pierogi is the flexibility you have in creating new and delicious fillings and toppings.

How to Make Pierogi - Overview

This is an overview of my pierogi making process. Some cooks will make the pierogi dough first. I prefer to prepare the filling first and refrigerate it while I make the dough. The reason for this is that no matter how careful you are in wrapping it, pierogi dough can dry out. If I have the filling made in advance, then once I prepare the dough I can quickly assemble the pierogi and not worry about the dough drying out.

So here is the process I follow.

1. Prepare the Filling in Advance.

   You can prepare it the same day or a day in advance. Put it in a bowl, wrap the bowl tightly with plastic wrap and refrigerate.

2. Prepare the Pierogi Dough

   Mix the pierogi dough according to the directions.

   Flour the work surface. Take 1/2 of the dough and put it on the work surface. Keep the remaining dough in a bowl covered in plastic wrap. Place a clean towel over the bowl.

   Using a rolling pin, roll out the dough on the work surface to 1/8" thickness. If you like thicker pierogi you can roll it to as much as 3/8" thickness.

Cut out 2 ½" to 3" circles using a round cookie cutter, a drinking glass or a pierogi cutter.

Stack the pierogi rounds on a plate with a small piece of wax paper between each round. Wrap the plate with plastic wrap as you continue to roll dough and cut out rounds.

3. Assemble the Pierogi Dough

Place 5 dough rounds on a floured work space.

Place a ball of filling on the center of each dough round. You can use a 1 tablespoon scoop which is 1/2 ounce. Or you can use a 3/4 ounce scoop for more filling. Make sure the filling is in the middle and doesn't go to the edge of the dough round.

There are several ways to seal a pierogi which I'll go into later. But this is a good, basic method.

With the pierogi round on a flat surface, fold the bottom edge of the dough up and over the filling until it lines up with the opposite edge of the dough. Pick the pierogi up and pinch the edges of the dough at the top together between your thumb and forefinger.

Then work your way around the edges pinching them together to seal them. If any filling moves to the edge before you seal the dough, press the filling back into the pierogi with a finger.

Go around the edge of the pierogi a second time and press the edges to make sure they're sealed. You can also press the tines of a fork around the edges of the pierogi to seal the dough and give it a fancier look.

If the dough edges don't seal together then apply some water on the inside edges of the dough and press to seal again.

Place each completed pierogi on a floured cookie sheet. Cover the cookie sheet with plastic wrap so that the pierogi don't dry out.

Combine any scraps of dough, roll them out and cut out more dough circles.

Complete this process for all of the dough in the bowl.

At this point you can follow the directions for boiling, sautéing, deep frying or baking the pierogi or you can freeze them.

How to Cut, Stuff & Seal Pierogi

Anyone who has made pierogi has their favorite ways of cutting, stuffing and sealing pierogi.

Method 1

This is the way my Grandmother made her pierogi. After she rolled out 1/2 of the pierogi dough to 1/8" she used a drinking glass to cut out 3" circles of dough.

Next she placed a 1 tablespoon scoop of filling in the middle of the dough round. Normally she had chilled the filling so it was easier to work with. She would brush the edge of the dough round with water or an egg wash so that it would seal better.

She picked up the dough round in her left hand. With her right forefinger she pressed the filling into the dough. At the same time with the thumb and forefinger of her left hand she stretched both sides of the dough up and over the filling. She sealed the dough at the top first. Then she sealed the sides by pinching the edges of the dough together. She always squeezed the edges of the pierogi together a second time to make sure there was no way the filling could leak out.

Method 2

My Mother rolls out the dough and uses either a drinking glass or a 3" round cookie cutter to cut out the rounds. She pulls up the scrap dough, forms it into a ball and puts it under plastic wrap.

She then puts a 1 tablespoon scoop of dough in the center of each pierogi round. She lightly brushes the edge of the dough rounds with a little egg wash. With the dough flat on the table, she pulls one edge of the dough up and over the filling and seals it with the opposite edge at the top. Then she picks the pierogi up and seals the edges with her thumb and forefinger. She also does a second squeezing of the edges to make sure they are sealed.

Method 3

When I was younger I cut, filled and sealed pierogi the way my Mother did. Then I discovered a couple of methods I liked better.

First my brother got a Zother Pierogi Cutter & Sealer and showed me how he made pierogi. I converted to his method because it was both easy and efficient.

First you roll out the dough. Then you put a line of three or four 1 tablespoon scoops of filling along the edge of the dough. The filling should be 1 ¼" away from the edge of the dough and there should be 1" between each scoop of filling.

Then you pull the edge of the dough up and over all of the scoops of filling. Press the dough down around the filling and between the scoops of filling.

Then you take the Zother Pierogi Cutter and sealer and position it over the first mound of filling. You want to cut a semicircle of dough that has the filling in the center and a dough border of 1/4" to 3/8". When you have the cutter positioned you press down until you cut through both the top layer of dough and the bottom layer of dough. If you peel away the excess dough around the pierogi you end up with a sealed pierogi with a crimped edge.

It only takes a few pierogi to get the hang of this method and you can usually fill, cut and seal pierogi faster than the hand method.

You can look at the Zother Pierogi Cutter at this site: http://www.buy.com/prod/round-ravioli-pierogi-cutter-sealer-stamp/225540404.html

Method 4

After I used the Zother cutter for a while I discovered the Pampered Chef Cut-N-Seal Cutter & Sealer. This cutter was originally developed to create homemade versions of Smuckers® Uncrustables® for children (sealed, crustless sandwiches with jelly fillings). But it works great with pierogi too.

Another thing I like about the Cut-N-Seal is the diameter is 3 ½" so I could make larger pierogi.

First you roll out the dough. Then you put a line of three or four 1 tablespoon scoops of filling along the edge of the dough. The filling should be 1 ¾ "in from the edge of the dough and there should be 1 ½ "between each scoop of filling.

Pull the edge of the dough up and over all of the scoops of filling. Press the dough down around the filling and between the scoops of filling.

Then you take the Cut-N-Seal and position it over the first mound of filling. You want to cut a semicircle of dough that has the filling in the center and a dough border of 1/4" to 3/8". When you have the cutter positioned you press down until you cut through both the top layer of dough and the bottom layer of dough. Twist the base of the cutter a little to make sure you've cut through the dough. Then depress the plunger all the way down to the base. This seals the pierogi and creates a nice, scalloped border.

You can look at the Cut-N-Seal at this site: http://www.amazon.com/gp/customer-media/product-gallery/B0016A680E/.

Method 5

I got the Hunky Bill large Pierogi Cutter & Sealer because it looked ingenious and produces 18 large pierogi quickly. Hunky Bill's Pierogi Cutter & Sealer.

I use this cutter and sealer when I'm making large batches of pierogi.

Place the wooden frame on your work surface. Flour the frame. Roll out two sheets of pierogi dough.

Drape the first sheet of dough over the frame. Put 1 ounce scoops of filling in each of the 18 depressions in the frame.

Drape the second piece of dough over the frame. Press down gently on the covered filling with your hands.

Take a rolling pin and roll it firmly over the top layer of dough. As you keep rolling the filling and dough will push down in the frame. When you see the outline of the frame around the pierogi you can stop rolling.

Remove the excess dough. Pick up the frame, turn it over, tap it on the work surface and you have 18 large filled and sealed pierogi. They also make a version for smaller pierogi but I prefer the larger model.

You can see the Hunky Bill Pierogi Cutter & Sealer on this site: http://www.amazon.com/100001-Big-Pierogi-Maker/dp/B00A4L9NEY/

How to Cook Pierogi

Most pierogi is traditionally boiled first. After that some pierogi are also sautéed. Savory pierogi like potato and sauerkraut are first boiled and then sautéed. They can also be deep fried. Some sweet pierogi like sweet cheese also taste great when boiled and then fried. However sweet fruit pierogi like strawberry, prune and blueberry are usually just boiled.

It's really a matter of taste though. For example in most recipes for Pierogi Ruskie the directions say to just boil the pierogi. But I have had Pierogi Ruskie that were first boiled and then fried and they were delicious.

There is also pierogi dough called Pierogi na Drozdach that includes a yeast leavening and is baked in the oven with the filling of your choice. The dough puffs up nicely and is delicious.

The directions for boiling, sautéing, deep frying and baking pierogi follow in the next sections.

Boiled Pierogi

This method works for both freshly made pierogi and frozen pierogi.

I've found the best approach is to use a large pot filled 3/4 with water. Add several tablespoons of salt and a tablespoon of cooking oil. The strategy is to cook the pierogi in small batches and to give them enough room so they don't touch and stick together. The oil helps to prevent the pierogi from sticking together.

Bring the pot of water to a roiling boil. Drop 6 to 8 pierogi 1 by 1 into the water. They'll drop to the bottom of the pot. Stir once with a wooden spoon to make sure they don't stick to the bottom. Don't put a cover on the pot.

When the pierogi rise to the surface cook them for 3 more minutes. Remove each pierogi with a slotted spoon. Let the water drain and transfer the pierogi to a cookie sheet that's been lightly coated with butter or vegetable oil.

Transfer to a serving platter with the garnish and sauces of your choice.

Sautéed Pierogi

My grandmother used to sauté savory pierogi in bacon fat. I've tried that and the taste is wonderful. If you sauté onion and top the pierogi with crumbled, crisp bacon and onions it's the perfect meal.

Normally though I sauté pierogi in butter with herbs and onions. I always boil the pierogi first and let them cool completely.

Here are the steps:

Boil the pierogi and let them cool completely.

Put 6 tablespoons of butter in a large, heavy-bottomed frying pan.

Sauté chopped onions in the pan until tender. Add any herbs you'd like.

Add the pierogi in the bottom of the pan so they're in one layer and not touching. Fry on medium heat for 4 to 5 minutes or until the bottoms of the pierogi are brown. Use a spatula to flip the pierogi and cook for 3 to 4 more minutes or until golden brown.

Transfer to a plate or serving platter and top with the onions.

Deep Fried Pierogi

We never had deep fried pierogi when I was growing up. But as an adult I have often served deep fried savory pierogi with excellent results.

Here are the steps:

Boil the pierogi, remove from the pot and let them cool completely.

Add enough olive oil to a deep pan or pot to so that you can completely submerge the pierogi.

When the oil is hot, carefully add 5 or 6 pierogi to the pan or pot. Keep the pierogi in the oil for several minutes. Turn the pierogi until they are browned. Remove the pierogi from the oil with a slotted spoon.

Transfer them to a plate or platter and pat with paper towels to remove any excess oil.

Serve with any topping appropriate to the filling.

Cook's Note:
I normally sauté any vegetables that I plan to serve with the pierogi. I prefer the taste and contrast of vegetables sautéed in butter to the pierogi deep fried in oil.

Baked Pierogi

When I was growing up we never had baked pierogi. Our pierogi was always boiled or fried. As an adult I was introduced to Pierogi na Drozdach which uses yeast dough. They are puffy and delicious after baking.

After doing more research I found that centuries ago in Poland there were traditional pierogi called Saniezki and Socznie that were also baked. These were small, sweet pierogi served on a person's Name Day.

In Poland today you'll find Pierogarnia which are restaurants that primarily serve pierogi. They sometimes have baked pierogi on their menus.

Some people prefer to bake other pierogi as well.   This is a matter of taste. I'd suggest experimenting with your favorite pierogi dough and fillings and see if you like the taste and texture of baked pierogi. I've tried this and prefer to not boil the pierogi before baking them.

Here's one way to bake pierogi. Preheat the oven to 400° F. Spray a cookie sheet with non-stick cooking spray. Put the pierogi on the cookie sheet taking care that they don't touch each other.   You can brush the pierogi with melted butter or olive oil. You can also brush with an egg wash (see below.)

Bake for 8 to 10 minutes. Flip them over at the halfway point.

Remove from the oven and allow cooling just a bit before serving.

Egg Wash #1

This will produce a flat golden brown color
1 egg
1 ½ Tbl water

Mix the egg and water together in a small bowl. Mix until frothy. Lightly brush the top of each pierogi with a thin coating of egg wash.

Egg Wash #2

The milk will produce a shiny, light brown color. The cream will produce a shiny, dark brown color. Half and Half will produce a shiny, golden brown color.

1 Tbl milk, half and half or cream

1 large egg yolk

Mix the egg yolk and milk (or half and half or heavy cream) together in a small bowl. Mix well. Lightly brush the top of each pierogi with a thin coating of egg wash.

How to Freeze Pierogi

You can easily freeze filled pierogi. I personally do not freeze raw pierogi dough. I've never found defrosted, raw pierogi dough to have the same softness and elasticity as fresh-made dough. However for those who want to try to freeze raw dough I include a method to try in Method 3 below.

There are a couple of ways to freeze filled pierogi.

Method 1

The first way is to take an airtight, freezer safe container like Tupperware® and line it with plastic freezer wrap. Lightly spray the bottom of the container with non-stick cooking spray. Put the pierogi in a single layer in the container. Lightly spray the pierogi with the non-stick cooking spray. Cover the pierogi with another layer of plastic freezer wrap. Spray this layer of freezer wrap with the non-stick cooking spray. Add another layer of pierogi. Continue with the layers of plastic wrap, spray and pierogi until the container is filled. Put the top on. Put the container in a freezer bag and put in the freezer. Label the bag with the date the pierogi were made

My sister uses this method but substitutes flour for the cooking spray.

Method 2

The second method involves blanching the pierogi in boiling water and then putting them into very cold water before freezing them.

Take a large pot of salted water with a tablespoon of cooking oil. Bring the water to a roiling boil. Drop 6 to 8 pierogi into the water one by one. Stir once with a wooden spoon to make sure they don't stick to the bottom. As soon as they pop to the top take them out with a slotted spoon and transfer them to a pot of ice cold water. Don't let the pierogi cook once they pop to the top of the pot.

Take the pierogi out of the cold water with a slotted spoon and put them on clean towels or paper towels to drain. Blot the pierogi with paper towels to remove any remaining water.

After drying the blanched pierogi, put them into Tupperware® containers as above and put in the freezer.

Although it's more work I use the blanching method. I see less cracking in the dough and I like the consistency of the dough once it's cooked.

Method 3

This is a method to freeze raw pierogi dough. After you've prepared the dough divide it into 8 smaller balls of dough. Double wrap each ball separately in heavy-duty plastic freezer wrap. Put the wrapped dough in freezer-ready plastic containers like Tupperware® and label them with the preparation date. Freeze pierogi dough for up to 1 month.

Cooking Frozen Pierogi

When I cook frozen pierogi I always transfer them to the refrigerator to defrost first. My frozen pierogi have always been blanched before freezing and I prefer the texture if I defrost them before boiling.

After defrosting the pierogi in the refrigerator I follow the steps listed in the Boiled Pierogi section. The same steps apply to frozen pierogi. Then if I plan to sauté or deep fry the pierogi I follow the steps in the Sautéed Pierogi or Deep Fried Pierogi sections.

Frozen pierogi can also be baked. Put the pierogi in a buttered baking dish. Cover the dish with aluminium foil. Bake at 400°F for 25 to 35 minutes or the filling is cooked through. Take the dish out of the oven. Drizzle some melted butter over the pierogi. Serve with your favorite toppings or sauce.

Cook's Note: Defrosting is a matter of taste. I know many people who don't defrost frozen pierogi before cooking and they are happy with the results.

PIEROGI DOUGH RECIPES

Pierogi Dough Overview

I've spoken to a lot of older Polish bakers including my Grandmother about pierogi dough. They often said that in their view that whole eggs or egg yolks shouldn't be added to the dough because it made it tougher. They continued to use a basic recipe of flour, water, oil and salt. This does produce nice, light dough.

My Mother, however, swears that her not-so-secret weapon of sour cream makes for lighter and more elastic dough. There's no argument that her pierogi dough is wonderful.

My view is that variety and experimentation is good. So in this section you'll find recipes for:

- traditional flour and water dough

- flour, butter and egg dough

- flour, egg, salt & water dough

- flour and sour cream dough

- flour, egg and sour cream dough

- flour, milk, water and oil dough

- flour, sour cream, cream cheese & butter dough

- Pierogi na Drozdach Yeast Doughs

- wheat flour dough

Experiment and find the dough that works best for you.

Important Note

In all of the recipes for pierogi dough, I provide the steps for working the dough by hand. You can certainly use any type of stand or hand mixer with a dough hook to blend and work the dough if you prefer that method.

Butter Pierogi Dough

This is wonderful dough for dessert pierogi like sweet cheese, strawberry or plum.   I've also used it successfully with savory pierogi fillings.

Yield: 50 to 60 Pierogi

Ingredients

1 cup unsalted butter
1 large egg
3/4 cup water, cold
4 ¼ cups all-purpose unbleached flour
1/4 tsp salt

Method

Melt the butter and let it cool slightly.

In a small bowl beat the egg. Add the water and mix completely.

Sift the flour into a large bowl.   Add the salt. Whisk to combine. Make a well or depression in the middle of the flour.

Pour the butter into the center of the flour. Then pour the egg mixture into the center of the flour. Use a fork or wooden spoon to mix the ingredients.

If the dough is sticky add a tablespoon of flour and knead. If it's still sticky add a little more flour and knead until the dough is soft and elastic.   If the dough feels hard and dry add a tablespoon of water and knead. If the dough is still not soft and smooth add a little more warm water and knead until the dough is soft and elastic.

Form the dough into a ball and put it into a large bowl. Cover the bowl with a clean towel and allow it to rest for 15 minutes.

When you're ready to make the pierogi, divide the dough into halves.   Wrap 1/2 of the dough with plastic wrap and return to the bowl.

Knead the dough half for 1 to 2 minutes.

Flour your work surface.   Put the 1/2 piece of dough on the work surface.   Use a rolling pin to roll the dough out to 1/8" thickness. If you like thicker pierogi you can roll it to as much as 3/8" thickness.

Cut out 3" circles using a round cookie cutter or glass.

Place a ball of filling on the center of each dough round. You can use a 1 tablespoon scoop which is 1/2 ounce. Or you can use a 3/4 ounce scoop for more filling.

Wet the inside edge of 1/2 of the pierogi dough with water or an egg wash.

Fold the dough in half over the filling and seal the edges with your fingers.   Press the edges a second time to make sure they're sealed. You can also press the tines of a fork around the edges of the pierogi to seal the dough and give it a fancier look.

If the dough doesn't seal apply some more water on the inside edges of the dough and press to seal again.

Place each completed pierogi on a cookie sheet. Cover the cookie sheet with plastic wrap so that the pierogi don't dry out.

Combine any scraps of dough, roll them out and cut out more dough circles.

Complete this process for all of the dough in the bowl.

At this point you can follow the directions for cooking the pierogi or you can freeze them.

Cream Cheese Pierogi Dough

This is wonderful dough for dessert pierogi like sweet cheese, strawberry or plum. I've also used it successfully savory pierogi fillings.

Yield: 36 Pierogi

Ingredients

1/2 cup sour cream
8 oz cream cheese, softened
8 oz unsalted butter, softened
1 tsp salt
3 ½ cups all-purpose unbleached flour

Method

Put a sheet of plastic wrap on the work area.

Put the sour cream, cream cheese and butter into a blender or food processor. Blend until smooth. Add the salt and pulse a few times.

Sift the flour into a medium bowl.

Add the flour 1 cup at a time to the butter-cheese mixture and pulse to blend.

After all of the flour has been added and combined, turn the dough out onto the sheet of plastic wrap.

Sprinkle your hands with flour and form the dough into a ball.

Tightly wrap the dough with the plastic wrap and chill overnight.

When you're ready to make the pierogi, divide the dough into halves. Wrap 1/2 of the dough with plastic wrap and return to the bowl.

Flour your work surface. Put the 1/2 piece of dough on the work surface. Use a rolling pin to roll the dough out to 1/8" thickness. If you like thicker pierogi you can roll it to as much as 3/8" thickness.

Cut out 3" circles using a round cookie cutter or glass.

Place a ball of filling on the center of each dough round. You can use a 1 tablespoon scoop which is 1/2 ounce. Or you can use a 3/4 ounce scoop for more filling.

Wet the inside edge of 1/2 of the pierogi dough with water.

Fold the dough in half over the filling and seal the edges with your fingers. Press the edges a second time to make sure there's a good seal. You can also press the tines of a fork around the edges of the pierogi to seal the dough and give it a fancier look.

If the dough doesn't seal apply some water on the inside edges of the dough and press to seal again.

Place each completed pierogi on a cookie sheet. Cover the cookie sheet with plastic wrap so that the pierogi don't dry out.

Combine any scraps of dough, roll them out and cut out more dough circles.

Complete this process for all of the dough in the bowl.

At this point you can follow the directions for cooking the pierogi or you can freeze them.

Dessert Pierogi Dough

This is great dough for dessert pierogi like sweet cheese, strawberry or plum.   I've also used it successfully with savory pierogi fillings.

Yield: 2 to 3 Dozen Pierogi

Ingredients

3 cups of all-purpose unbleached flour
1/2 tsp salt
3/4 cup of hot milk
1/4 cup of cold water
1/2 tsp cooking oil

Method

Sift the flour into a large bowl.   Add the salt. Make a well or depression in the middle of the flour.

Pour the hot milk into the center of the flour. Stir with a fork so that the flour and milk combine. Eliminate as many lumps as you can. You can also use your hands to mix the dough.

Cover the bowl with a clean towel. Set aside for 5 minutes.

Pour the cold water into the bowl and mix into the dough with a fork. You can again use your hands to mix and knead the dough.

Cover the bowl with the towel and let the dough rest for 15 minutes.

After 15 minutes pour the cooking oil onto the dough and knead it in. Knead for 5 to 10 minutes. The dough should be smooth and soft. Form the dough into a ball and put back into the bowl. Cover with a towel and let it rest another 15 minutes.

When you're ready to make the pierogi, divide the dough into halves. Wrap 1/2 of the dough with plastic wrap and return to the bowl.

Flour your work surface. Put the 1/2 piece of dough on the work surface. Use a rolling pin to roll the dough out to 1/8" thickness. If you like thicker pierogi you can roll it to as much as 3/8" thickness.

Cut out 3" circles using a round cookie cutter or glass.

Place a ball of filling on the center of each dough round. You can use a 1 tablespoon scoop which is 1/2 ounce. Or you can use a 3/4 ounce scoop for more filling.

Wet the inside edge of 1/2 of the pierogi dough with water or an egg wash.

Fold the dough in half over the filling and seal the edges with your fingers. Press the edges a second time to make sure they're sealed. You can also press the tines of a fork around the edges of the pierogi to seal the dough and give it a fancier look.

If the dough doesn't seal apply some more water on the inside edges of the dough and press to seal again.

Place each completed pierogi on a cookie sheet. Cover the cookie sheet with plastic wrap so that the pierogi don't dry out.

Combine any scraps of dough, roll them out and cut out more dough circles.

Complete this process for all of the dough in the bowl.

At this point you can follow the directions for cooking the pierogi or you can free them.

Pierogi na Drozdach Yeast Dough #1

Pierogi dough is usually unleavened and is boiled and then optionally fried. Pierogi na Drozdach is a leavened version that is baked and puffs up more than traditional unleavened pierogi dough. This type of raised dough is great with meat, potato, cheese or cabbage fillings. I haven't used it for fruit fillings yet.

Yield: 2 Dozen Pierogi

Ingredients

1/2 cup milk
1/2 envelope dry yeast
1 tsp sugar
5 Tbl flour
2 eggs, lightly beaten
2 ½ cups unbleached flour
1 tsp salt
1/4 cup butter

Method

Sift the flour into a medium bowl.

Scald 1/2 cup of milk. Pour the milk into a large bowl. Allow the milk to cool to lukewarm.

Pour 1/2 packet of yeast into the lukewarm milk.

Add the sugar and 5 Tbl of sifted flour to the yeast mixture. Beat the ingredients well. The batter should be loose like crepe batter. If it's too thick add a little more milk.

Cover the bowl with a clean towel and put in a warm place to rise, approximately 15 minutes.

After the yeast mixture has risen, add the lightly beaten eggs to the yeast mixture. Stir to mix.

Add the remaining sifted flour and salt to the yeast mixture. Work the flour until it forms into a dough. Knead the dough well.

Add a little butter to the dough and continue kneading until the butter is absorbed. Keep adding butter and kneading until the butter is gone.

The dough should be smooth and soft.

Put the dough into a bowl. Cover the bowl with a towel and put it in a warm place to rise until it doubles in size – approximately 1 hour.

After the dough has doubled, preheat the oven to 350° F.

Spray a cookie sheet with non-stick baking spray.

Take 1/2 of the dough out of the bowl and put it on a floured surface. Be sure to cover the remaining dough in the bowl.

Roll the dough out to 3/8" thickness. Use a round cookie cutter or glass to cut out 3" rounds of dough.

Place a ball of filling on the center of each dough round. You can use a 1 tablespoon scoop which is 1/2 ounce. Or you can use a 3/4 ounce scoop for more filling.

Brush the inside edge of the dough round with water or an egg wash.

Fold the dough in half over the filling and seal the edges with your fingers. Press the edges a second time to make sure they're sealed. You can also press the tines of a fork around the edges of the pierogi to seal the dough and give it a fancier look.

Place each completed pierogi on a cookie sheet. Allow enough space between them since they will rise again.   Cover the cookie sheet with plastic wrap so that the pierogi don't dry out.

Combine any scraps of dough, roll them out and cut out more dough circles.

Complete this process for all of the dough in the bowl.

Once you've prepared all the pierogi let them all rest on the cookie sheet for 1/2 hour.

Preheat the oven to 350° F.

Put the pierogi in the oven and bake for 25 to 35 minutes or until golden brown.

Pierogi na Drozdach Yeast Dough #2

This version of pierogi na drozdach adds sour cream for a different taste and texture.

Yield: 3 to 4 dozen Pierogi

Ingredients

4 eggs
1 Tbl melted butter
1 tsp salt
1 package active dry yeast
1/4 cup warm water
1 Tbl sugar
1 cup sour cream
4 cups all-purpose flour

Method

In a medium bowl beat the eggs, melted butter and salt until fluffy and thick.

Add the yeast to the warm water in a large bowl. Allow to stand for 10 minutes.

Add the egg mixture to the yeast. Beat in the sugar and sour cream.

Sift the flour into a large bowl.

Add the flour 1 cup at a time to the yeast mixture. Stir to combine. Keep adding flour until the dough is firm.

Put the dough on a floured board and knead for 3 minutes. Put the dough in a greased bowl. Cover with a towel or plastic wrap. Put the bowl in a warm place for 1 hour. The dough should double in volume.

Preheat the oven to 350° F.

Spray a cookie sheet with non-stick baking spray.

Take 1/2 of the dough out of the bowl and put it on a floured surface. Be sure to cover the remaining dough in the bowl or it will dry out.

Roll the dough out to 3/8" thickness. Use a round cookie cutter or glass to cut out 3" rounds of dough.

Place a ball of filling on the center of each dough round. You can use a 1 tablespoon scoop which is 1/2 ounce. Or you can use a 3/4 ounce scoop for more filling.

Brush the inside edge of the dough round with water or an egg wash.

Fold the dough in half over the filling and seal the edges with your fingers. Press the edges a second time to make sure they're sealed. You can also press the tines of a fork around the edges of the pierogi to seal the dough and give it a fancier look.

Place each completed pierogi on a cookie sheet. Allow enough space between them since they will rise again. Cover the cookie sheet with plastic wrap so that the pierogi don't dry out.

Combine any scraps of dough, roll them out and cut out more dough circles.
Complete this process for all of the dough in the bowl.
Once you've prepared all the pierogi let them all rest on the cookie sheet for 1/2 hour.

Preheat the oven to 350° F.

Put the pierogi in the oven and bake for 25 to 35 minutes or until golden brown.

Simple Pierogi Dough

This is a simple water-based Pierogi Dough recipe using just 4 ingredients.

Yield: 2 to 3 Dozen Pierogi

Ingredients

2 to 2 ½ cups all-purpose unbleached flour
1 large egg
1 tsp salt
About 1 cup warm water

Method

Heat the water in the microwave and then set it aside until the water is warm to the touch.

Sift 2 cups of flour into a large bowl. Make a hole or well in the center of the flour.

Crack the egg into the well and add the salt. Add a little bit of the warm water.   Mix initially with a fork. Work the dough with your hands, adding a little more water at a time. Knead the dough until it's smooth and soft.

If the dough is sticky add a tablespoon of flour and knead. If it's still sticky add a little more flour. If the dough feels hard and dry add a tablespoon of water and knead. If the dough is still not soft and smooth add another tablespoon of warm water and knead.

When the dough is done, form it into a round and wrap with plastic wrap. Put the dough in a bowl and cover with a clean towel.

Allow the dough to rest for 10 to 20 minutes.

Divide the dough in half.

Roll to a thickness of 1/8" on a floured board. If you like thicker pierogi you can roll it to as much as 3/8" thickness.

Use a large round cookie cutter or a large glass to cut out circles of dough. The circles should be approximately 3 inches in diameter.

Place a ball of filling on the center of each dough round. You can use a 1 tablespoon scoop which is 1/2 ounce. Or you can use a 3/4 ounce scoop for more filling.

Wet the inside edge of 1/2 of the pierogi dough with water.

Fold the dough in half over the filling and seal the edges with your fingers. Press the edges a second time to make sure they're sealed. You can also press the tines of a fork around the edges of the pierogi to seal the dough and give it a fancier look.

Place each completed pierogi on a cookie sheet. Cover the cookie sheet with plastic wrap so that the pierogi don't dry out.

Combine any scraps of dough, roll them out and cut out more dough circles.

Complete this process for all of the dough in the bowl.
At this point you can follow the directions for cooking the pierogi or you can freeze them.

Sour Cream Pierogi Dough

This is wonderful pierogi dough that works with both savory and sweet fillings.

Yield: 1 to 2 Dozen Pierogi

Ingredients

2 cups all-purpose unbleached flour
1/2 tsp salt
1 large egg
1/2 cup sour cream
1/4 cup butter softened

Method

Sift the flour and salt together into a large bowl.   Form a well in the middle of the flour. Beat the egg and add it to the flour mixture.

Add the sour cream and softened butter to the flour mixture. Knead the dough for 3 to 5 minutes. The dough shouldn't be sticky. If it is sticky add a tsp of flour to the dough and knead it until it's smooth and feels soft. Continue adding small amounts of flour until you have dough that is smooth and soft.

Wrap the dough in plastic wrap and refrigerate for at least 30 minutes. 24 hours is ideal.

When you're ready to make the pierogi, divide the dough into halves. Wrap 1/2 of the dough with plastic wrap.

Flour your work surface. Put the 1/2 piece of dough on the work surface. Use a rolling pin to roll the dough out to 1/8" thickness. If you like thicker pierogi you can roll it to as much as 3/8" thickness.

Cut out 3" circles using a round cookie cutter or glass.

Place a ball of filling on the center of each dough round. You can use a 1 tablespoon scoop which is 1/2 ounce. Or you can use a 3/4 ounce scoop for more filling.

Wet the inside edge of 1/2 of the pierogi dough with water.

Fold the dough in half over the filling and seal the edges with your fingers. Press the edges a second time to make sure they're sealed. You can also press the tines of a fork around the edges of the pierogi to seal the dough and give it a fancier look.

Place each completed pierogi on a cookie sheet. Cover the cookie sheet with plastic wrap so that the pierogi don't dry out.

Combine any scraps of dough, roll them out and cut out more dough circles.

Complete this process for all of the dough in the bowl.

At this point you can follow the directions for cooking the pierogi or you can free them.

Sour Cream Pierogi Dough #2

This is great dough that works with both savory and sweet fillings.

Yield: 3 to 4 Dozen Pierogi

Ingredients

3 cups all-purpose unbleached flour
1 egg
1 cup water, warmed
1/2 tsp salt
1/4 cup sour cream

Method

Heat the water in a microwave until it's hot. Set it aside until the water is warm to the touch.

Sift the flour and salt into a large bowl. Make a well in the middle of the flour.

Crack the egg into a medium bowl. Beat well.   Add the egg to the well in the middle of the flour.

Add the warm water and sour cream to the flour.

Mix the flour until the dough holds together. It should be smooth and soft.

If the dough is dry just add water a tablespoon at a time until it's moist. If the dough is sticky add more flour, a tablespoon at a time, until it's smooth.

On a floured work surface, knead dough for 3 or 4 minutes until elastic. Cover dough with plastic wrap and refrigerate for at least 30 minutes.

When you're ready to roll out the dough, cut off approximately 1/2 of the dough in the bowl. Leave the remaining dough covered in plastic wrap.

Roll out the portion of dough you have on a floured work surface until its 1/8" thick. If you like thicker pierogi you can roll it to as much as 3/8" thickness.

Cut out 3" dough rounds with a round cookie cutter or drinking glass.

Place a ball of filling on the center of each dough round. You can use a 1 tablespoon scoop which is 1/2 ounce. Or you can use a 3/4 ounce scoop for more filling.

Wet the inside edge of 1/2 of the pierogi dough with water.

Fold the dough in half over the filling and seal the edges with your fingers. Press the edges a second time to make sure they're sealed. You can also press the tines of a fork around the edges of the pierogi to seal the dough and give it a fancier look.

Place each completed pierogi on a cookie sheet. Cover the cookie sheet with plastic wrap so that the pierogi don't dry out.

Combine any scraps of dough, roll them out and cut out more dough circles.

Complete this process for all of the dough in the bowl.

At this point you can follow the directions for cooking the pierogi or you can free them.

Cook or freeze the pierogi.

Traditional Egg-free Pierogi Dough

My Grandmother and her friends never used eggs in their pierogi dough. They felt dough without eggs was lighter and tasted better after cooking. So here is a traditional egg-free recipe for pierogi dough.

Yield: 2 to 3 Dozen Pierogi

Ingredients

3 cups of all-purpose flour
3/4 cup of boiling water
1/4 cup of cold water
1/2 tsp salt
1/2 tsp cooking oil

Method

Sift the flour into a large bowl. Add the salt. Make a well or depression in the middle of the flour.

Pour the boiling water into the center of the flour. Stir with a fork so that the flour and water combine. Eliminate as many lumps as you can.

Cover the bowl with a clean towel. Set aside for 5 minutes.

Pour the cold water into the bowl and mix into the dough with a fork. You can also use your hands to mix the dough.

Cover the bowl with the towel and let the dough rest for 15 minutes.

After 15 minutes pour the olive oil onto the dough and knead it in. Knead for 5 to 10 minutes. The dough should be smooth.

Divide the dough into halves. Wrap 1/2 of the dough with plastic wrap and return it to the bowl.

Flour your work surface. Put the 1/2" piece of dough on the work surface. Use a rolling pin to roll the dough out to 1/8" thickness. If you like thicker pierogi you can roll it to as much as 3/8" thickness.

Cut out 3" circles using a round cookie cutter or glass.

Place a ball of filling on the center of each dough round. You can use a 1 tablespoon scoop which is ½ ounce. Or you can use a 3/4 ounce scoop for more filling.

Wet the inside edge of 1/2 of the pierogi dough with water.

Fold the dough in half over the filling and seal the edges with your fingers. Press the edges a second time to make sure they're sealed. You can also press the tines of a fork around the edges of the pierogi to seal the dough and give it a fancier look.

Place each completed pierogi on a cookie sheet. Cover the cookie sheet with plastic wrap so that the pierogi don't dry out.

Combine any scraps of dough, roll them out and cut out more dough circles.

Complete this process for all of the dough in the bowl.

At this point you can follow the directions for cooking the pierogi or you can freeze them.

Wheat Pierogi Dough

This is great dough for dessert pierogi like sweet cheese, strawberry or plum. I've also used it successfully with some other savory pierogi fillings.

Yield: 2 to 3 Dozen Pierogi

Ingredients

3 cups wheat flour
3/4 cup boiling water
1/4 cup cold water
1/2 tsp salt
1/2 tsp cooking oil

Method

Sift the flour into a large bowl. Add the salt. Make a well or depression in the middle of the flour.

Pour the boiling water into the center of the flour. Stir with a fork so that the flour and milk combine. Eliminate as many lumps as you can. You can also use your hands to mix the dough.

Cover the bowl with a clean towel. Set aside for 5 minutes.

Pour the cold water into the bowl and mix into the dough with a fork. You can again use your hands to mix and knead the dough.

Cover the bowl with the towel and let the dough rest for 15 minutes.

After 15 minutes pour the cooking oil onto the dough and knead it in. Knead for 5 to 10 minutes. The dough should be smooth and soft. Form the dough into a ball and put back into the bowl. Cover with a towel and let it rest another 15 minutes.

When you're ready to make the pierogi, divide the dough into halves. Wrap 1/2 of the dough with plastic wrap and return to the bowl.

Flour your work surface. Put the 1/2 piece of dough on the work surface. Use a rolling pin to roll the dough out to 1/8" thickness. If you like thicker pierogi you can roll it to as much as 3/8" thickness.

Cut out 3" circles using a round cookie cutter or glass.

Place a ball of filling on the center of each dough round. You can use a 1 tablespoon scoop which is 1/2 ounce. Or you can use a 3/4 ounce scoop for more filling.

Wet the inside edge of 1/2 of the pierogi dough with water.

Fold the dough in half over the filling and seal the edges with your fingers. Press the edges a second time to make sure they're sealed. You can also press the tines of a fork around the edges of the pierogi to seal the dough and give it a fancier look.

Place each completed pierogi on a cookie sheet. Cover the cookie sheet with plastic wrap so that the pierogi don't dry out.

Combine any scraps of dough, roll them out and cut out more dough circles.

Complete this process for all of the dough in the bowl.

At this point you can follow the directions for cooking the pierogi or you can free them.

PIEROGI FILLING RECIPES

SAVORY PIEROGI FILLINGS

Beef Filling

This is a tasty mixture of beef, garlic, cream cheese, Monterey Jack and Cheddar Cheese.

Yield: 3 cups of Pierogi Filling

Ingredients

1 large onion, minced
2 Tbl butter
1 ½ lbs ground beef
1 clove garlic, crushed with garlic press
1 Tbl chopped parsley
salt to taste
pepper to taste
3 oz cream cheese, cut into 1" cubes
1/4 cup Monterey Jack cheese shredded
1/4 cup Mild Cheddar Cheese shredded

Method

Lightly sauté the onion in the butter. Add the ground beef and crushed garlic to the onions. Stir well. Cook until the beef has browned. Drain the beef well.

Add the parsley, salt and pepper to the ground beef and stir well.

Add the cream cheese to the beef and stir until combined. Add the Monterey and Cheddar cheeses. Mix well until the cheeses are melted and blended with the beef.

Remove from the heat. Cool well before using.

Cool completely. Wrap and refrigerate until you're ready to prepare the pierogi.

Beef Serrano Pepper Filling

This is a spicy combination of beef, garlic and Serrano hot peppers. You can substitute 2 jalapeno peppers for the Serrano pepper. This will give you a milder pepper taste.

Yield: Filling for 2 to 3 dozen pierogi

Ingredients

1 Serrano pepper
1 medium onion, peeled
1 clove garlic
2 Tbl extra virgin olive oil
2 lbs ground beef
1 large egg, lightly beaten
salt to taste
pepper to taste

Method

Use plastic gloves when preparing the Serrano pepper.

Wash the Serrano pepper. Slice it in two length-wise and remove the seeds. Finely chop the pepper.

Slice and finely chop the onion.

Mince the garlic.

Add the olive oil to large frying pan. Add the Serrano pepper, onion and garlic to the pan. Sauté the vegetables on low heat until the onions are translucent and the pepper and garlic are soft.

Remove the mixture from the heat and cool completely.

Put the ground beef into a large bowl. Add the beaten egg, salt and pepper to the beef and mix well.

Add the Serrano pepper mixture to the beef.

Mix well with a large wooden spoon.

Cool completely. Wrap and refrigerate until you're ready to prepare the pierogi.

Cabbage Filling

This is a great filling for both regular pierogi dough and the Yeast Dough Pierogi.

Yield: 3 cups of Pierogi Filling

Ingredients

1 large onion
3 Tbl butter
3 cups finely shredded cabbage
1 cup mushrooms, finely chopped
salt to taste
pepper to taste
1 package (8 oz) cream cheese
2 Tbl chopped fresh dill

Method

Finely chop the onion and sauté it in the butter until it is golden. Add the cabbage, mushrooms, salt and pepper. Cover the pan and cook the vegetables over a low flame, stirring occasionally, for about 1/2 hour.

Let the mixture cool slightly.

Transfer the vegetables to a large bowl. Add the softened cream cheese and dill. Mix well until combined.

Cool completely. Wrap and refrigerate until you're ready to prepare the pierogi.

Cheddar Kielbasa Filling

This is a filling that's great when the pierogi is boiled and then fried.

Yield: Filling for 2 to 3 Dozen Pierogi

Ingredients

2 lbs smoked kielbasa

1 cup onion, finely diced

1 Tbl extra virgin olive oil

1/8 tsp thyme

1/8 tsp rosemary

1 cup mild cheddar cheese, shredded

Method

Remove the casing from the kielbasa. Finely dice the sausage. Put the olive oil, kielbasa and onion in a large frying pan.

Sauté the kielbasa and onions on medium heat until browned.

Remove from the heat and add the thyme and rosemary. Stir well.

Add the shredded cheddar cheese and stir until the cheese is melted.

Cool completely. Wrap and refrigerate until you're ready to prepare the pierogi.

Chorizo Chipotle Filling

This is a contemporary and spicy pierogi filling.

Yield: Filling for 2 Dozen Pierogi

Ingredients

1 lb chorizo

1 tsp chipotle chile pepper, minced **

1/2 onion, diced

2 cloves of garlic, minced

2 Tbl butter

5 russet potatoes peeled and boiled

8 oz cheddar cheese, shredded

Method

In a large skillet crumble and cook the chorizo. Drain any grease and set aside.

Use plastic gloves before handling the pepper. Remove 1 chipotle pepper and rinse off the adobo sauce with water. Slice lengthwise and remove any seeds. Rinse in water again. Finely mince the chipotle pepper.

Sauté the chipotle pepper, onion and garlic in a little bit of butter just until onion is translucent. Set aside.

Mash the potatoes in a large bowl.

Add the chipotle pepper, onions and garlic, chorizo and cheddar cheese. Mix well.

Cool completely. Wrap and refrigerate until you're ready to prepare the pierogi.

Cook's Note:

** You can buy small cans of chipotle peppers in adobo sauce. You can also freeze any leftover sauce and peppers. I use a plastic ice cube tray. I put the sauce into separate cube partitions. I put the peppers in a food processor and pulse the peppers until they're shredded. Spoon portions of the peppers in separate ice cube partitions. Put the tray of peppers in a freezer bag. Freeze until you need more peppers.

Mushroom Filling

This is a vegetarian filling that families in Poland would serve at the meatless Christmas Eve dinner. With this filling I usually make the pierogi dough first.

Yield: Filling for 3 dozen Pierogi

Ingredients

3 cups finely chopped fresh mushrooms

5 Tbl butter

2 large finely chopped onions

5 Tbl fine dry breadcrumbs

Salt and pepper to taste

Method

Sauté the mushrooms and onions in butter in a large skillet. Sauté until the mushrooms and onions are tender.

Remove from the heat and cool.

Add the breadcrumbs, salt and pepper. Mix well until the bread crumbs are incorporated.

Use immediately.

Pierogi Ruskie Filling

Pierogi Ruskie can be served warm after boiling, topped with caramelized onions, crisp minced bacon and sour cream. You can also grill or fry them after boiling for a different texture.

By the way Ruskie refers to Ruthenia (ancient Rus) which over time has included different portions of Eastern Europe. In modern times it would include portions of Belarus, northern Ukraine, western Russia, small parts of northeastern Slovakia and narrow strips of eastern Poland

Yield: Filling for 30 Pierogi

Ingredients

2 lbs russet potatoes
1 large onion, finely chopped
8 oz room-temperature farmers cheese or pressed cottage cheese or ricotta cheese
1 tsp sugar
1 egg yolk, beaten
Salt to taste
Pepper to taste

Method

Peel the potatoes. Cut them in half. Cook them in boiling water until tender. Remove from the water and cool in a bowl.

Sauté the onions in 1 tablespoon of butter until golden brown.

Press the potatoes through a potato press or ricer into a large bowl.

If using pressed cottage cheese, press the cheese through the potato press or ricer. If using either farmers cheese or ricotta cheese just add it to the potatoes.

Add the sautéed onions, sugar, beaten egg yolk, salt and pepper to the potatoes and cheese.

Use a spoon to mix until all of the ingredients are incorporated.

Use one hand to complete blending the filling.

Cool completely. Wrap and refrigerate until you're ready to prepare the pierogi.

Cook's Note:

It's important to salt and pepper this filling to taste. If the filling is unseasoned it can taste bland.

Potato Cheese Filling With Mint

This is a regional Polish pierogi filling.

Yield: Filling for 30 pierogi

Ingredients

2 lbs russet potatoes, peeled and quartered
1/2 cup butter
1/4 cup fresh mint leaves, finely chopped
4 oz cream cheese
3 oz sour cream
1 tsp white pepper
salt to taste
1 lb farmers cheese or pressed cottage cheese, room
temperature

Method

Add water and 2 tablespoons salt to a large pot. Add the
potatoes to the pot. Bring the water to a boil.

When the potatoes are tender, drain the water from the pot.
Transfer the potatoes to a large mixing bowl.

Add the butter, chopped mint leaves, cream cheese, sour cream, pepper and salt into the bowl and mix on a medium speed. Mix until smooth.

If using pressed cottage cheese put the cottage cheese through a potato press or ricer. If using farmer cheese don't use a potato press or ricer.

Add the farmers cheese or pressed cottage cheese to the potato mixture.

Mix on high for several minutes until fluffy. Salt to taste.

Cool completely. Wrap and refrigerate until you're ready to prepare the pierogi.

Potato & Basil Filling

This is a basic potato pierogi filling with fresh garlic and basil. But the great thing about this filling is you can customize it with whatever spices and added ingredients you normally like with potatoes.

Here are just a few suggestions: bacon, basil, Cajun spice, chives, cilantro, dill, grated cheddar, horseradish, lemon pepper, minced garlic, mint, nutmeg, oregano, paprika, parsley, pepper, roasted garlic, rosemary, salt, thyme.

Yield: Filling for 4 cups Pierogi

Ingredients

1 cup onion, finely chopped
4 Tbl butter
1 tsp finely minced garlic
1 tsp basil
1 tsp salt
1/2 tsp pepper
4 cups russet or Yukon gold potatoes, mashed or riced

Method

In a large skillet or pot, sauté the onion in the butter for 5 minutes, stirring periodically. Add the minced garlic, basil, salt and pepper. Stir well and heat for 2 more minutes.

Add the potatoes to the onion mixture. Stir to combine the potatoes with the onions, garlic and spices. The mixture should be well-blended. Cook for 10 to 15 minutes.

Remove from the heat.

Cool completely. Wrap and refrigerate until you're ready to prepare the pierogi.

Potato & Jalapeno Filling

This is a spicy, contemporary Pierogi Filling.

Yield: Filling for 2 to 3 Dozen Pierogi

Ingredients

2 ½ lbs Idaho potatoes, cooked and mashed
1/4 cup unsalted butter, cut into small pats
2 Tbl jalapeno peppers, seeds removed and finely chopped
1 medium onion, peeled and finely chopped
3 garlic cloves, peeled and finely chopped
2 Tbl butter for sautéing
1 lb cheddar cheese, grated
1 tsp salt to taste
pepper to taste

Method

Put the hot mashed potatoes in a large bowl. Add the butter
and continue to mash until the butter is melted and blended

In a medium pan sauté the jalapeno peppers, onions and
garlic until they're golden brown.

Add the sautéed jalapeno peppers, onions and garlic to the
mashed potatoes.
Add the cheddar cheese to the mashed potatoes. Mix until all
of the ingredients are combined.
Salt and pepper to taste.

Cool completely. Wrap and refrigerate until you're ready to prepare the pierogi.

Potato & Two Cheese Filling

This is a wonderful, cheese-filled Pierogi Filling.

Yield: 6 cups Pierogi filling

Ingredients

4 large russet potatoes, peeled and quartered
3/4 cup butter
2 medium onions, chopped
8 oz room-temperature farmers cheese or pressed cottage cheese
8 oz grated cheddar cheese
Salt and pepper

Method

Cook potatoes until tender.   Drain the pot and transfer the potatoes to a bowl to cool.

Put the butter and onions in a large skillet. Sauté the onion slowly at low temperature for 15 to 20 minutes. The onions will turn golden brown and will caramelize. Stir frequently.

Press the potatoes through a potato press or ricer into a large bowl. As an alternative you can mash the potatoes.

If using pressed cottage cheese put the cottage cheese through a potato press or ricer. If using farmer cheese don't use a potato press or ricer.

Add the cottage cheese or farmer cheese to the potatoes.

Add the grated cheddar cheese, salt and pepper.

Add the caramelized onions to the potatoes. Mix well until the potatoes, cheese, salt and pepper are all well-blended.

Cool completely. Wrap and refrigerate until you're ready to prepare the pierogi.

Potato, Sauerkraut & Bacon Filling

This is one of my favorite, traditional Pierogi Fillings.

Yield: Filling for 2 to 3 Dozen Pierogi

Ingredients

2 ½ lbs russet potatoes
1/2 lb bacon
1 cup sauerkraut
1 whole yellow onion, peeled
2 Tbl butter
1 cup sharp shredded cheddar cheese
1/2 tsp salt
1/2 tsp pepper

Method

Peel and quarter the potatoes. Boil the potatoes in salted water until tender.

Drain the potatoes and place in a large bowl. Cool for 15 minutes.

Press the cooled potatoes through a ricer into a large bowl. (Instead of using a ricer you can mash the potatoes but it's important to get rid of all lumps.)

Put the bacon into a large skillet and turn the heat to medium-low. Turn the bacon over frequently so that both sides are cooked evenly.   If too much bacon fat collects in the skillet pour it off and continue cooking. Keep cooking until the bacon is deep brown.

Remove the skillet from the heat. Put the bacon on a plate covered with a paper towel. Blot the top of the bacon with more paper towel. When all of the grease has been blotted up transfer the bacon to a clean plate and let it cool.

Crumble the cooled bacon into a medium bowl. Set aside.

Rinse the sauerkraut in water and squeeze out as much moisture as you can.   Blot with clean paper towels. Finely chop the sauerkraut.

Grate the onion.

Add 2 Tbl butter to a large skillet or pot. Add the potatoes to the skillet or pot.

Add the chopped sauerkraut and onion to the mashed potatoes. Stir to mix.

Add the bacon, cheddar cheese, butter, salt and pepper to the potato-sauerkraut mixture. Mix thoroughly.

The mixture should be thick but spreadable. You can add a small amount of milk if the mixture becomes overly dense.

Cool completely. Wrap and refrigerate until you're ready to prepare the pierogi.

Sauerkraut & Mushroom Filling

This is a traditional Polish Pierogi Filling.

Yield: Filling for 2 to 3 Dozen Pierogi

Ingredients

2 cups sauerkraut
1 small onion, finely chopped
3 Tbl butter
2 cups mushrooms
Salt & pepper
3 Tbl sour cream
1 hard-boiled egg, chopped

Method

Rinse the sauerkraut in cold water.   Squeeze out as much of the water as you can.

Finely chop the sauerkraut.

In a large skillet sauté the onion in the butter until they're golden brown.

Finely chop the mushrooms.   Add the mushrooms to the skillet with the onions. Cook for 2 minutes.

Add the sauerkraut to the skillet and mix with the onions and mushrooms. Add the salt and pepper.   Stir to mix. Fry for 20 minutes or until the sauerkraut becomes golden brown.

Remove the skillet from the heat. Add the sour cream and chopped egg and stir well.

Cool completely. Wrap and refrigerate until you're ready to prepare the pierogi.

Sauerkraut & Onion Filling

This is another traditional Polish Pierogi Filling.

Yield: Filling for 2 to 3 Dozen Pierogi

Ingredients

1 lb sauerkraut
1 large chopped onion
4 Tbl butter
3 Tbl sour cream
1 tsp dill
salt and pepper

Method

Rinse the sauerkraut in cold water. Squeeze the moisture out of the sauerkraut.

Finely chop the sauerkraut.

In a large skillet cook the onion in the butter until tender. Add the sauerkraut.   Cook for 5 to 10 minutes until the sauerkraut is cooked through.

Take the skillet off of the burner.

Stir in the sour cream, dill, salt and pepper.

Take 1 Tbl of the mixture and form a small ball. If the mixture doesn't hold its shape add a little more sour cream.

Cool completely. Wrap and refrigerate until you're ready to prepare the pierogi.

Spinach Cheese Filling

This is another traditional pierogi filling. This is another filling where you can add your favorite spices.

Yield: Filling for 2 to 3 Dozen Pierogi

Ingredients

2 cups fresh spinach leaves, chopped
2 garlic cloves, finely chopped
1 Tbl extra virgin olive oil
2 cups ricotta cheese
1 tsp lemon pepper
Salt to taste

Method

Wash the spinach well.   Finely chop the spinach.

Finely chop the garlic.   Add the olive oil and garlic to a small frying pan.   Using low heat, sauté the garlic until it softens. Stir with a wooden spoon so that the garlic doesn't burn.

Remove the garlic from the heat and cool completely.

To a large bowl add the ricotta cheese, spinach and cooled garlic mixture. Stir well so that the cheese, spinach and garlic are combined.

Add the lemon pepper and salt.

Cool completely. Wrap and refrigerate until you're ready to prepare the pierogi.

SWEET PIEROGI FILLINGS

Apple Filling

This is a wonderful sweet apple pierogi.

Yield: Filling for 3 to 4 Dozen Pierogi

Ingredients

3 large apples (Fuji or Gala are good)
1 Tbl lemon juice
1 tsp cinnamon (optional)
1 ½ cups granulated sugar

Method

Peel and core the apples. Finely chop the apples until you have 3 cups.
Put the chopped apples in a large bowl.

Sprinkle the apples with the lemon juice. Sprinkle the cinnamon over the apples. Toss the apples.

Wrap the bowl of apples and refrigerate while you prepare the pierogi dough.

Assemble the Apple Pierogi
Take the apples out of the refrigerator.

Put the sugar in a medium bowl.

Place 1 teaspoon to 1 tablespoon of apple filling in the middle of each dough round.

Top the apples with 1/4 teaspoon sugar.

Fold and seal the pierogi with your fingers.

Place each completed pierogi on a cookie sheet and cover with plastic wrap.

When all of the pierogi have been prepared, follow the directions for boiling the pierogi. Don't fry the apple pierogi.

Blackberry Filling

This is a great dessert pierogi.

Yield: Filling for 3 to 4 dozen pierogi

Ingredients

3 cups fresh whole blackberries
1 cup granulated sugar

Method

Wash and clean the blackberries. Put them in a large bowl.

Wrap the bowl in plastic wrap and refrigerate the berries until the pierogi dough has been prepared.

Assemble the Blackberry Pierogi

Take the blackberries out of the refrigerator.

Put the sugar in a medium bowl.

Place 1 teaspoon to 1 tablespoon of blackberry filling in the middle of each dough round.

Top the blackberries with 1/4 teaspoon sugar.

Fold and seal the pierogi with your fingers.

Place the completed pierogi on a cookie sheet and cover with plastic wrap.

When all of the pierogi have been prepared, follow the directions for boiling the pierogi. Don't fry the blackberry pierogi.

Prune Filling

Mom uses the Cream Cheese pierogi dough for prune pierogi. These are great topped with melted butter, granulated sugar or powdered sugar

Yield: Filling for 3 dozen prune pierogi

Ingredients

2 cups dried, pitted prunes
1 Tbl lemon juice
1 Tbl brown sugar
1 tsp cinnamon

Method

Put the prunes in a saucepan and cover with water. Heat the prunes uncovered on medium heat. When the water starts to boil, add the lemon juice, brown sugar and cinnamon. Cover the pan and remove from the heat. Let the prunes steep for 20 to 30 minutes.

Drain the prunes and refrigerate until the pierogi dough has been prepared.

Assemble the Prune Pierogi

Take the prunes out of the refrigerator.

Place 1 prune in the middle of each dough round.

Fold and seal the pierogi with your fingers.

Place the completed pierogi on a cookie sheet and cover with plastic wrap.

When all of the pierogi have been prepared, follow the directions for boiling the pierogi. Don't fry the prune pierogi.

Raspberry Filling

This is another wonderful dessert pierogi. Although it's a good choice for lunch or a light dinner.

Yield: Filling for 3 to 4 dozen pierogi

Ingredients

3 cups fresh whole raspberries
1 cup granulated sugar

Method

Wash and clean the raspberries. Put the raspberries in a large bowl.

Wrap the bowl in plastic wrap and refrigerate the berries until the pierogi dough has been prepared.

Assemble the Raspberry Pierogi
Take the raspberries out of the refrigerator.

Put the sugar in a medium bowl.

Place 1 teaspoon to 1 tablespoon of raspberry filling in the middle of each dough round.

Top the raspberries with 1/4 teaspoon sugar.

Fold and seal the pierogi with your fingers.

Place the completed pierogi on a cookie sheet and cover with plastic wrap.

When all of the pierogi have been prepared, follow the directions for boiling the pierogi. Don't fry the raspberry pierogi.

Strawberry Filling

Strawberries are one of my favorite fruits. I love Strawberry Pierogi.

Yield: Filling for approximately 3 dozen pierogi

Ingredients

1 lb fresh strawberries
1 to 2 cups granulated sugar
1 Tbl flour

Method

Let the strawberries sit out at room temperature for an hour.

Clean each strawberry well with a wet paper towel. It's best to avoid rinsing strawberries because they're porous and absorb water.

Remove the stems with a paring knife.

Cut the strawberries into 1/4 or 1/8 portions. Put them in a large bowl.

Pour several teaspoons of sugar over the strawberries. Mix gently. Cover the bowl and set aside while you make the dough.

Assemble the Strawberry Pierogi

After the dough has been prepared and cut into rounds, take the cover off the bowl of strawberries. Stir them gently.

Add the flour to the strawberries and stir so that the flour is combined.

Put 1 teaspoon of the strawberries in the center of a dough round. Sprinkle 1/4 teaspoons of sugar over the strawberries.

Moisten the inside edges of the dough round with water or an egg wash. Fold 1 end of the dough over the filling and press the edges with your fingers to seal the dough. Press the edges together a second time to make sure the strawberries can't leak out during cooking.

Boil the pierogi as explained in the How to Cook Pierogi – Boiled Pierogi section. Don't fry Strawberry Pierogi.

After cooking transfer them to a bowl and sprinkle them with melted butter.

Serve with honey butter or regular butter, whipped cream & nuts.

Sweet Cheese Filling

This is one of my favorite sweet pierogi and can be served with a variety of homemade fruit sauces.

Yield: 2 cups of Pierogi Filling

Ingredients

2 cups farmers cheese or ricotta cheese
3 oz cream cheese, softened
1 large egg, beaten
2 Tbl melted unsalted butter
3 Tbl sugar
1 tsp vanilla
1/4 cup golden raisins

Method

Put the cheese in a large bowl.   Use a mixer to mix the cheese until it's smooth.

Add the softened cream cheese and mix until smooth and blended.

Add the beaten egg, butter, sugar and vanilla to the cheese mixture.   Use the mixer on the high setting to completely blend the cheese mixture.

Stir in the golden raisins.

Wrap tightly with plastic wrap and chill for at least 2 hours.

Serve with apple sauce, raspberry sauce, lemon sauce, vanilla yogurt or any fruit sauce

PIEROGI TOPPINGS

TRADITIONAL PIEROGI TOPPINGS

Buttered Bread Crumbs

This is a traditional Polish topping. Sprinkle the buttered bread crumbs over warm pierogi.

Ingredients

1/2 cup dry bread crumbs
4 Tbl melted butter
1/2   tsp salt
1/4 tsp pepper

Method

Add the bread crumbs to a medium bowl.

Pour the melted butter over the bread crumbs.

Add the salt and pepper to the bread crumbs

Stir to mix until the butter is incorporated

Caramelized Onions

Ingredients

4 large Vidalia onions
1/4 cup unsalted butter, softened

Method

Peel the onions and quarter them.   Finely slice each quarter.

In a large frying pan add the butter and onions. Sauté the onions for 2 to 3 minutes on medium-low heat.

It's important to stir the onions until they're golden brown.

Remove from the heat.

Fried Bacon

Ingredients

1 lb thickly sliced bacon

Method

In a large frying pan lay out rows of the sliced bacon. Cook on medium-low heat until browned.

Stir the bacon and turn the slices over periodically. Cook until the bacon is crispy.

If you like to fry pierogi in bacon fat you can pour the bacon fat into a container. Otherwise, discard the bacon fat.

Blot the bacon with paper towels.

Crumble the bacon.

Sour Cream & Sugar Topping

Ingredients

1 cup sour cream
1 Tbl brown sugar or to taste
pinch of salt

Method

Mix all of the ingredients well and serve on top with sweet pierogi.

Cook's Note: White granulated sugar can be substitutes for the brown sugar.

Other Traditional Toppings

These are some of the toppings that my Mother and Grandmother served with the pierogi they made. My Grandmother's pierogi normally came with sour cream, onions and bacon. My Mother enjoys experimenting with butter and different herbs and spices, both for frying pierogi and topping pierogi.

Savory Toppings
Caramelized Onions
Applesauce
Crisp crumbled bacon
Melted butter
Melted butter & chives
Melted butter & fried onions
Melted butter & parsley
Onions fried in bacon fat
Sour cream
Sour Cream & chives

Sweet Toppings
Applesauce
Granulated sugar
Powdered sugar
Sour cream
Thickened cream with vanilla sugar
Whipped cream

CONTEMPORARY PIEROGI TOPPINGS

Onion & Kielbasa Pierogi Topping

I have served this topping both with the casing removed from the sausage and with it left on. Experiment to see which version you like better.

Ingredients

3 cups smoked kielbasa, chopped
1 cup green onions, chopped
1 clove garlic, minced
Butter for frying
salt to taste
pepper to taste

Method

Add the butter and kielbasa to a large frying pan and cook for 5 minutes.

Add the onion and garlic.

Sauté until golden brown.

Serve over a plate of pierogi with a side dish of sour cream.

Yogurt Garlic Pierogi Topping

This is a delicious topping with a little spicy kick to it.

Ingredients

1 cup plain yogurt
1 clove garlic, minced
2 tsp lemon juice, freshly squeezed
2 tsp sugar
1/2 tsp hot pepper flakes

Method

Add the yogurt and garlic to a medium bowl. Mix well.

Add the lemon juice, sugar and hot pepper flakes. Stir well.

If you'd like it spicier add a little more hot pepper flakes.

Serve on the side with the pierogi.

Other Contemporary Pierogi Toppings

If contemporary pierogi fillings are limited only by your imagination, then the same is true of toppings that you put over boiled, fried or baked pierogi. These are just a few ideas.

Caramelized onions and chopped kielbasa
Caramelized onions, butter & paprika
Caramelized onions, sage, and jalapeno
Caramelized onions, finely chopped bacon, and garlic
Cream cheese and chives
Melted cheddar cheese
Sour cream & chopped green onions
Sour Cream, chives & garlic
Sour Cream, fresh basil, & green onion
Yogurt, garlic & herbs

COMPOUND BUTTER TOPPINGS

Compound butters are a homemade mixture of butter with herbs, spices or fruit.

It's important to start with softened butter that has been sitting at room temperature for a while. The butter should be soft but not melted.

If you plan to make a lot of compound butters there are commercial butter molds you can buy. If you're crafty you can make your own butter mold out of wood. Or you can use other containers like fluted mini cupcake pans.

Herb Butter

This is a homemade compound herb butter that's easy to make and is delicious over savory pierogi.

Ingredients

1/2 cup unsalted butter, very soft
pinch of salt
1 Tbl minced rosemary
1 Tbl minced sage
1 Tbl minced thyme

Method

Place the softened butter in a medium bowl. Whip the butter with a mixer. Add a pinch of salt.

Add the rosemary, sage and thyme. Use a rubber spatula or a mixer to fold and mix until spices are completely incorporated. You want an even distribution of spices throughout the butter.

Turn the butter out on a piece of plastic wrap. Use the wrap to help form the butter into a log about 6 inches long. Wrap the log in the plastic wrap. Twist the ends of the plastic wrap and use a plastic tie to secure each end.

Allow the wrapped butter to sit in a cool spot for 1 hour. Then refrigerate for at least 2 hours before serving for better flavor.

Honey Butter

Honey butter is delicious over sweet pierogi.

Ingredients

1/2 cup unsalted butter, very soft
1/2 cup honey

Method

Place the softened butter in a medium bowl. Use a mixer to whip the butter.

Add the honey. Use a rubber spatula or a mixer to fold and mix the honey until it's completely incorporated. You want an even distribution of honey and butter.

Turn the butter out on a piece of plastic wrap. Use the wrap to help form the butter into a log about 6 inches long. Wrap the log in the plastic wrap. Twist the ends of the plastic wrap and use a plastic tie to secure each end.

Allow the wrapped butter to sit in a cool spot for 1 hour. Then refrigerate for at least 2 hours before serving for better flavor.

Horseradish Butter

Horseradish butter works best with savory pierogi especially with potato and kielbasa fillings.

Ingredients

1/2 cup unsalted butter, very soft
3 Tbl horseradish
1/3 cup chives, chopped
Dash ground black pepper

Method

Place the softened butter in a medium bowl. Use a mixer to whip the butter.

Add the horseradish and chopped chives to the bowl. Use a rubber spatula or mixer to fold and mix the butter, horseradish, chives and pepper until they are completely incorporated. You want an even distribution of horseradish and chives throughout the butter.

Turn the butter out on a piece of plastic wrap. Use the wrap to help form the butter into a log about 6 inches long. Wrap the log in the plastic wrap. Twist the ends of the plastic wrap and use a plastic tie to secure each end.

Allow the wrapped butter to sit in a cool spot for 1 hour. Then refrigerate for at least 2 hours before serving for better flavor.

Lemon Butter

This is a homemade compound lemon butter that's easy to make and is wonderful over both sweet and savory pierogi.

Ingredients

1/2 cup unsalted butter, very soft
Zest of 1/2 lemon
1 Tbl lemon juice, freshly squeezed
1/4 tsp black pepper

Method

Place the softened butter in a medium bowl. Use a mixer to whip the butter.

Add the lemon zest, lemon juice, minced garlic and pepper to the butter. Use a rubber spatula or mixer to mix the lemon zest, lemon juice and pepper until they are completely incorporated. You want an even distribution of lemon juice and zest throughout the butter.

Turn the butter out on a piece of plastic wrap. Use the wrap to help form the butter into a log about 6 inches long. Wrap the log in the plastic wrap. Twist the ends of the plastic wrap and use a plastic tie to secure each end.

Allow the wrapped butter to sit in a cool spot for 1 hour. Then refrigerate for at least 2 hours before serving for better flavor.

Lemon Garlic Butter

Lemon Garlic butter is delicious over many savory pierogi.

Ingredients

1/2 cup unsalted butter, very soft
2 cloves garlic, finely chopped
Zest of 1/2 lemon
1 tsp lemon juice, freshly squeezed
1/4 tsp black pepper

Method

Place the softened butter in a medium bowl. Use a mixer to whip the butter.

Add the garlic, lemon zest, lemon juice and pepper to the butter. Use a rubber spatula or mixer to mix the garlic, lemon zest, lemon juice and pepper until they are completely incorporated. You want an even distribution of garlic and lemon throughout the butter.

Turn the butter out on a piece of plastic wrap. Use the wrap to help form the butter into a log about 6 inches long. Wrap the log in the plastic wrap. Twist the ends of the plastic wrap and use a plastic tie to secure each end.

Allow the wrapped butter to sit in a cool spot for 1 hour. Then refrigerate for at least 2 hours before serving for better flavor.

Mustard Tarragon Butter

This is a homemade compound herb butter that's easy to make and is wonderful over savory pierogi especially potato pierogi.

Ingredients

1/2 cup butter, softened
2 Tbl fresh tarragon, chopped
1 ½ tsp Dijon mustard
freshly ground black pepper

Method

Place the softened butter in a medium bowl. Use a mixer to whip the butter.

Add the tarragon, mustard and pepper to the butter. Use a rubber spatula or mixer to mix the tarragon, mustard and pepper until they are completely incorporated. You want an even distribution of tarragon and mustard throughout the butter.

Turn the butter out on a piece of plastic wrap. Use the wrap to help form the butter into a log about 6 inches long. Wrap the log in the plastic wrap. Twist the ends of the plastic wrap and use a plastic tie to secure each end.

Allow the wrapped butter to sit in a cool spot for 1 hour. Then refrigerate for at least 2 hours before serving for better flavor.

Rosemary Garlic Butter

Rosemary Garlic butter is wonderful with savory pierogi.

Ingredients

1/2 cup unsalted butter, very soft
1 Tbl fresh rosemary, chopped
2 cloves garlic, very finely chopped
1/4 tsp salt
1/4 tsp black pepper

Method

Place the softened butter in a medium bowl. Use a mixer to whip the butter.

Add the rosemary, garlic, salt and pepper to the butter. Use a rubber spatula or mixer to mix the rosemary, garlic, salt and pepper until they are completely incorporated. You want an even distribution of garlic and rosemary throughout the butter.

Turn the butter out on a piece of plastic wrap. Use the wrap to help form the butter into a log about 6 inches long. Wrap the log in the plastic wrap. Twist the ends of the plastic wrap and use a plastic tie to secure each end.

Allow the wrapped butter to sit in a cool spot for 1 hour. Then refrigerate for at least 2 hours before serving for better flavor.

Vanilla Bean Butter

Vanilla Bean butter is so good on all sweet pierogi.

Ingredients

1/2 cup unsalted butter, very soft
1 vanilla bean

Method

Place the softened butter in a medium bowl. Use a mixer to whip the butter.

Split the vanilla bean lengthwise. Scrape out the seeds and add them to the butter. Discard the pod. Use a rubber spatula or mixer to mix the vanilla bean seeds until they are completely incorporated with the butter. You want an even distribution of vanilla throughout the butter.

Turn the butter out on a piece of plastic wrap. Use the wrap to help form the butter into a log about 6 inches long. Wrap the log in the plastic wrap. Twist the ends of the plastic wrap and use a plastic tie to secure each end.

Allow the wrapped butter to sit in a cool spot for 1 hour. Then refrigerate for at least 2 hours before serving for better flavor.

Vanilla Cinnamon Butter

Vanilla Cinnamon butter is especially good on apple pierogi. It works well with other sweet pierogi too.

Ingredients

1/2 cup unsalted butter, very soft
1 vanilla bean
1 tsp cinnamon

Method

Place the softened butter in a medium bowl. Use a mixer to whip the butter.

Split the vanilla bean lengthwise. Scrape out the seeds and add them to the butter. Discard the pod.

Add the cinnamon to the butter. Use a rubber spatula or mixer to mix the vanilla bean seeds and cinnamon until they are completely incorporated with the butter. You want an even distribution of vanilla and cinnamon throughout the butter.

Turn the butter out on a piece of plastic wrap. Use the wrap to help form the butter into a log about 6 inches long. Wrap the log in the plastic wrap. Twist the ends of the plastic wrap and use a plastic tie to secure each end.

Allow the wrapped butter to sit in a cool spot for 1 hour. Then refrigerate for at least 2 hours before serving for better flavor.

SAUCES

Lemon Sauce

This is an excellent lemon sauce that works well with sweet or savory pierogi.

Yield: 1 ½ cups

Ingredients

1/2 cup granulated sugar
1 Tbl cornstarch
1/4 tsp salt
1 cup boiling water
2 Tbl fresh lemon juice
1 Tbl finely grated lemon zest
1 Tbl butter

Method

In a large saucepan, combine the sugar, cornstarch and salt. Stir to combine.

Slowly add the boiling water. Cook over low heat and stir frequently until the sauce thickens.

Remove from heat. Stir in the lemon juice, lemon peel and butter.

This sauce is best served warm over warm pierogi.

Raspberry Sauce

This is a thicker raspberry sauce with chunks of raspberry that is a perfect topping for Sweet Cheese Pierogi.

Yield: 2 cups

Ingredients

4 cups fresh raspberries, divided

1 cup sugar

2 tsp lemon juice

1 cup water

2 Tbl cornstarch

Method

Pour 2 cups of the raspberries into a medium bowl. Use a potato masher to crush the raspberries and break them down. Transfer the raspberries and any juice to a large saucepan.

Add the sugar and lemon juice to the raspberries in the saucepan.

Bring the mixture to a simmer.

Add the water and cornstarch to a small bowl. Whisk until well-mixed.

Add the cornstarch mixture to the raspberries in the saucepan. Stir the raspberry mixture for 1 to 2 minutes or until it thickens.

Remove from the heat and fold in the remaining 2 cups of raspberries.

Cool before using.

Strawberry Sauce

This is a thick strawberry sauce with chunks of strawberries that is delicious.

Yield: 2 cups

Ingredients

2 cups strawberries, washed, hulled, and diced
1 cup granulated sugar
1/2 cup water
1 tsp lemon zest, finely grated
1 Tbl lemon juice, freshly squeezed
1 Tbl cornstarch

Method

Put 1 cup of the strawberries into a medium saucepan. Use a potato masher to crush the strawberries.

Add 1/2 cup of sugar to the strawberries in the saucepan. Mix the crushed strawberries and sugar until the strawberries are covered with sugar.

Add the remaining 1 cup of strawberries, 1/2 cup sugar, water, and lemon juice and lemon zest.   Stir until the sugar is incorporated.

Bring the strawberry mixture to a boil. Once it boils reduce the heat to medium.   Cook for 5 to 10 minutes or until the strawberries break down. Use the potato masher to further break down the strawberries.

If you see any foam on top of the sauce skim it off.

Mix the cornstarch with 3 tablespoons of water. Add the cornstarch mixture to the strawberries. Increase the heat to high and stir for 5 minutes or until the sauce thickens.

Remove from the heat. Cool the sauce tin a bowl before using.

Basil Cheese Sauce

Basil is one of my favorite herbs. This sauce is excellent on most savory pierogi.

Yield: 2 cups

Ingredients

2 cups fresh basil leaves
4 cloves garlic, minced
1/4 cup olive oil
1/4 cup walnuts, toasted and chopped
1/2 cup Parmesan cheese, grated
1/2 cup Romano cheese, grated
1 salt and pepper to taste
1 pint light cream

Method

Add the basil and garlic to a blender or food processor. Blend the basil and garlic and slowly add the olive oil. Blend for 40 to 60 seconds.

Add the walnuts, Parmesan, Romano, salt and pepper. Blend for 1 minute or until smooth.

In a large saucepan heat the cream on low until it simmers.

Add 1/2 of the hot cream into the blender or processor with the basil-cheese mixture. Pulse for 20 to 30 seconds until the ingredients are combined.

Pour the basil mixture back into the saucepan and simmer until it thickens – usually for 5 minutes.

Dill Sauce

Dill is another wonderful herb. This sauce is great on most savory pierogi.

Yield: 2 cups

Ingredients

1 ½ cups sour cream
1 ½ cups mayonnaise
1/4 tsp salt
1/4 tsp pepper
1 tsp dill weed
1 tsp prepared horseradish
1 Tbl lemon juice

Method

Mix all of the ingredients in a blender until smooth and creamy.

Refrigerate until ready to use.

Sour Cream Chive Sauce

This sauce has a traditional feel to it and is excellent with savory pierogi.

Yield: 2 cups

Ingredients

3 Tbl butter
2 cloves garlic, finely chopped
2 Tbl flour
1 ¾ cup chicken broth
1/2 tsp salt
1/4 tsp white pepper
1/4 cup sour cream
1/3 cup chives

Method

In a large pan heat the butter over medium heat.

Add the garlic to the pan and cook it until it softens and turns yellow. Stir the garlic constantly. Don't overcook or brown it.

Add the flour and stir until it is well absorbed by the butter and garlic. Keep stirring until the mixture turns yellow.

Slowly stir in the chicken broth until the sauce is thick and smooth.

Add the salt and pepper.   Add in the sour cream and whisk until smooth.

Right before serving add the chives.

Mailing List

Would you like to receive individual recipes from me or learn in advance how to get my next book at a discount?

If you would, then please join my mailing list by entering the link below into your Web browser. It will take you to the page on Amazon where you can leave a review. Enter the following link:

https://landing.mailerlite.com/webforms/landing/t6c0h7

I promise I won't ever send you spam because I hate receiving it myself.

To send me an email: RoseWysocki@gmail.com

Thank you very much.

Rose Wysocki

About the Author

~

Rose Wysocki and her husband live near Boston. They both come from Polish families who immigrated to Massachusetts in the early 1900's. Rose grew up in a family of 6 children who were all steeped in Polish traditions by their parents and grandparents. They were raised on traditional Polish cooking. From an early age Rose and her brothers and sisters would help stuff and seal pierogi. When she got older Rose helped her mother make different pierogi fillings.

Rose passed on traditional Polish cuisine to her own 4 children. She really enjoys combining traditional pierogi fillings with contemporary toppings, flavored butters and sauces. She has also loves to combine contemporary fillings with traditional pierogi dough.

When her grandchildren get a little older she plans to introduce them to the joy of Polish cooking.

Books by Rose Wysocki

Perfect Pierogi Recipes

Perfect Polish Dessert Recipes

Perfect Polish Appetizer Recipes

Made in the USA
Middletown, DE
05 July 2023

34570512R00113